# LAND PRESERVATION

## A TRUE BOOK®

by
**Christine Petersen**

**Children's Press®**
A Division of Scholastic Inc.

New York  Toronto  London  Auckland  Sydney
Mexico City  New Delhi  Hong Kong
Danbury, Connecticut

*Reading Consultant*
**Jeanne Clidas**
*State University of*
*New York College*

*Content Consultant*
**Jacqueline Geoghegan**
*Clark University*

A California housing
development encroaches
on nearby vineyards.

Library of Congress Cataloging-in-Publication Data

Petersen, Christine.
  Land preservation / Christine Petersen.
    p. cm. — (A true book)
Summary: Discusses how human use of land and increasing population
have threatened natural landscapes and describes the establishment of
national parks as a means of preserving these resources.
Includes bibliographical references (p.   ) and index.
  ISBN 0-516-22806-4 (lib.bdg.)     0-516-21940-5 (pbk.)
  1. National parks and reserves—History. 2. Forest reserves—History—
Juvenile literature. 3. Biosphere reserves—History—Juvenile literature.
4. Environmental protection—History—Juvenile literature. 5. Land trusts—
History—Juvenile literature. [1. Conservation of natural resources. 2. National
parks and reserves.] I. Title. II. Series.
  SB481.3.P48 2003
  333.78'09—dc22
                                    2003018342

CHILDREN'S PRESS, and A TRUE BOOK®, and associated logos are trademarks and or registered trademarks of Scholastic Library Publishing.
SCHOLASTIC and associated logos are trademarks and or registered trademarks of Scholastic Inc.
1 2 3 4 5 6 7 8 9 10 R 13 12 11 10 09 08 07 06 05 04

# Contents

The first colonists in North America cut down trees to build homes.

# Taming the Wilderness

When European people first
arrived on the North American
continent in the early 1500s,
they found a wilderness covered
in forests so thick that they
could hardly be walked through.
Marshes and grasslands
stretched as far as the eye
could see. Native people lived

on the land, but left few signs of their presence.

Lured by this bountiful land, thousands of people immigrated (moved) across the Atlantic Ocean to the American colonies. They quickly began to "tame" the wilderness, cutting down forests for firewood and lumber and to make room for farms and towns.

By 1800, the land between the Atlantic Ocean and the Mississippi River was as crowded

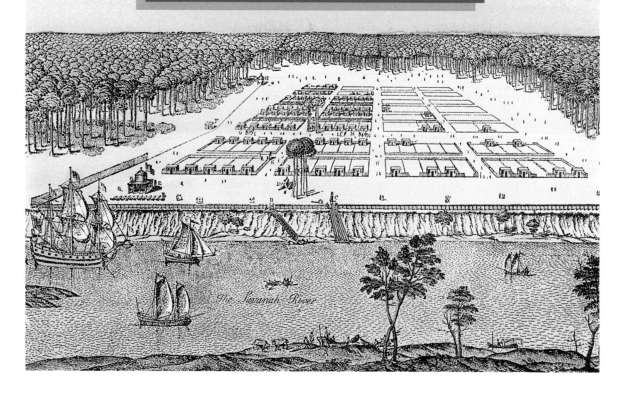

Large tracts of land were cleared as the colonies grew in size.

The Savannah River

with people as it once had been with trees. To meet the need for open land, the United States government sent explorers to investigate the western half of

The open space and majestic scenery of the West attracted many pioneers.

the continent, known as the "Wild West." Word came back that the West was filled with wildlife, open spaces, valuable minerals, and few people. Restless pioneers quickly began crossing the Mississippi to set up homesteads.

Soon, immigrants had settled all the land between the Atlantic and Pacific oceans. Thousands of miles of railroad were built across the heart of the country from east to west.

Gulch mining in the Old West

Loggers cutting down trees

Lumber companies cut down whole forests. Miners dug into mountains in search of valuable minerals such as silver and gold. Hunters and trappers killed off bison, wolves, and other wildlife.

Some Americans began to realize that the nation's great wilderness was in trouble. They began to think about ways to **preserve** this land, before it was too late.

# Why Preserve Land?

In 2002, more than 287 million people lived in the United States—and that number grows by at least 3 million every year. As the nation's population increases, so does our demand for land. Forests, fields, and marshes are still being cleared every day to make room for

A contour strip farm in Wisconsin

homes and farms. We continue
to dig up mountains and prairies
to find **natural resources** such as
oil, gas, minerals, and metals.
All over the world, land is being
"eaten up" to meet the needs of
humans. As a result, the planet's

13

Rivers and lakes support Earth's living things (top). A fern thrives in rich soil (bottom left). A giraffe eats from a tree (bottom right).

wild natural places are steadily being chipped away.

Although we may not notice it, humans need nature in order to survive. Rivers and lakes contain fresh water for drinking. Soils work to filter and store rainwater, and they provide the nutrients and homes that plants need to grow. In turn, animals eat plants, microscopic creatures, and other animals. This food web is one of the reasons why so many species, or different kinds of living things, can share our planet.

When humans replace natural landscapes with cities and highways, the damage reaches far beyond the land itself. Cities are full of cars and factories, which produce air **pollution**. These toxic chemicals rise into the **atmosphere** and mix with water, then fall back to Earth as acid rain. As a result, plants and animals in even

What was once a natural environment is now the city of New York, with tall buildings, cars, and pollution.

the world's hardest-to-reach places can suffer from pollution poisoning.

# This Land Is Your Land

President Abraham Lincoln took the first step in protecting our nation's wilderness. In 1864, he asked Congress to donate glacier-carved Yosemite Valley and a nearby grove of ancient redwood trees to the state of California. As a park, all people would be able to enjoy the beauty of Yosemite.

In 1872, President Ulysses S. Grant made history when he signed a bill creating the world's first official **national park**, Yellowstone. Located in the northwestern corner

Buffaloes are one of many kinds of animals that live in Yellowstone National Park (above). A crowd gathers to watch the Old Faithful geyser erupt in Yellowstone National Park (right).

of Wyoming (as well as parts of Idaho and Montana), Yellowstone has sharp mountain peaks that tower over lush green forests. Grizzly bears, bison, and wolves wander the plains, and natural fountains called geysers spew hot water high into the air.

National parks ensure that America's most precious natural wonderlands are protected from logging, mining, and other damaging activities. Today, the National Parks System pre-serves more than 365 parks, battlefields, cemeteries, sea-shores, trails, and other sites that are of scientific and historic value to our nation. For example, the Grand Canyon and the Petrified Forest reveal how the land has changed over millions of years. Mesa Verde and Canyon of the Ancients contain cliff dwellings and buildings made by Native Americans more than a thousand years ago.

At the same time that they preserve our lands, national parks can sometimes feel like amusement parks. More than

The layers of rock revealed in the Grand Canyon were formed at different times in Earth's history.

275 million people visit U.S. national parks each year, creating traffic jams, noise, and pollution that harm the parks' air, water, and wildlife.

# Roosevelt's Legacy

Roosevelt's passion for the environment had a great impact on America.

President Theodore Roosevelt believed that the treasures found on public land belong to the American people and should not be harmed. During his years as president, from 1901 to 1909, Roosevelt worked hard to preserve our nation's land and resources. He established five new national parks and eighteen national monuments to safeguard natural wonders and historic places. Roosevelt also set aside fifty-five wildlife refuges to preserve the habitats of important wild animals.

# Land of Many Uses

In 1905, President Roosevelt created the National Forest Service to manage one of America's most important resources—its forests. His friend Gifford Pinchot was chosen to lead the organization.

Pinchot was convinced that it is possible to use America's

Gifford Pinchot worked with Roosevelt to make the environment a national issue.

natural resources wisely, while also protecting the environment. He saw the National Forest System as a different kind of park: a "land of many uses." **National forests** would continue to provide homes for the plants and animals that had always lived there. People could visit to camp, ski, fish, and hike. At the same time, businesses would pay the federal government to collect trees, minerals, or water, or to graze livestock inside the forest boundaries.

This was not a new idea. For centuries, kings and governments have set up parks to manage land and resources. England's New Forest is a good example. In 1079, King William the Conqueror made a large section of forest on England's southern coast into a hunting park—only members of the king's court could hunt deer and wild pigs within its boundaries. But peasants living nearby continued to farm, graze cattle, and collect plants from the forest. Today, the New Forest still contains some of the largest woodlands, grasslands, and bogs in England.

England's New Forest (above) and William the Conquerer (right)

# Ecotourism

**M**ost of us spend time in parks built by the cities, counties, and states in which we live. But ecotourism, or traveling to see the world's natural places, has now become popular, too. Ecotourism is a big business that can benefit nature. Although it can be expensive to start new parks, poorer nations have discovered that wildlands can be good sources of income. Instead of using up land to make money, countries such as Costa Rica have preserved their forests and coastlines to attract visitors. People come from around the world to see rare animals and plants and to be close to nature. The money collected from tourists pays for the parks, and the tourism industry provides many jobs for local people.

Tourists cross a canopy walkway in Costa Rica's Santa Elena Cloud Forest.

# Parks for the Future

In recent years, parks and pre-serves have sprung up in nations around the world. Yet **environmentalists** are still concerned. Most parks are like small "islands," surrounded by cities and farms. Because the land around them is already in use, these parks can never grow larger. Animals living within them cannot travel far without crossing paths with humans.

Environmentalists prefer to set aside large blocks of wilderness that are unbroken by roads, towns, or farms. In such areas, people are not allowed to drive vehicles, hunt, farm, or build towns. Such protection gives species, resources, and beautiful places a better chance to remain wild long into the future.

The United Nations has a program that works toward this

A boat gently navigates Sian Ka'an Biosphere Reserve in Mexico.

goal by setting up biosphere reserves. (*Biosphere* is a word that includes all living things and their environments.) These reserves are created in natural areas that are important to wild animals and plants, local people, nations, and the world. The center of each biosphere reserve, called the "core area," contains the most carefully protected land. Inside the core area, no human activity— hunting, logging, or building— is allowed. Surrounding the core area is a wide belt of land called a "buffer zone," inside which local people can fish and hunt. Around it all, a third layer includes villages, farms, and recreation areas.

The Maya Biosphere Reserve helps protect endangered species such as the scarlet macaw.

Guatemala's Maya Biosphere Reserve is one of 425 biosphere reserves found around the world. Covering more than 7,720 square miles (20,000 square kilometers),

Maya contains seven core areas that protect lakes, rivers, swamps, and one of the world's northernmost tropical rain forests. In the buffer zone, local people gather wood and plants for food and medicine. Half a million people live right outside the Maya Biosphere Reserve, many of whom have jobs working in the reserve. Another 180,000 ecotourists come to Maya every year to enjoy its beauty and wildness.

# The World's Largest Park

**T**o visit the world's largest park, you'll have to put on your warmest clothes and fly north of the Arctic Circle to the island of Greenland. North East Greenland National Park contains 375,290 square

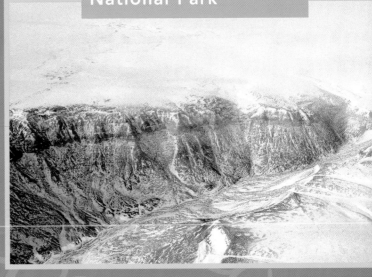

North East Greenland National Park

miles (972,000 square kilometers), an area about the size of Texas and New Mexico put together. It's a land of tundra, glaciers, mountains, and shorelines that is home to polar bears, walruses, and caribou—but very few humans. To protect the region's healthy wilderness, Greenland law allows only the country's native Inuit people, scientific research teams, and a few travelers inside the park each year.

# You Can Preserve, Too!

Governments and international organizations have the power and money to preserve the great wildernesses of the world, but individuals can make a difference, too.

The Nature Conservancy is one of many private organizations involved in land preservation. It buys blocks of land from people

Wildflowers are protected in Minnesota's Bluestem Prairie Preserve (above). A conservation corps member plants oak trees (left).

and businesses all over the world, in order to protect endangered habitats—seashores, marshes, grasslands, deserts, and rain forests. The organization also helps governments and businesses learn ways to keep land safe for the future.

Land trust organizations are another way to conserve privately owned land. A land trust helps its members legally protect their land so that it may never be sold to businesses or developed into towns. When many people living side by side form a land trust, large areas can be preserved for the future. Sonoma Land Trust in northern California is a wonderful

California is home to some of the world's tallest trees—redwoods.

example. Over the past twenty-seven years, Sonoma Land Trust has helped preserve 15,000 acres of beautiful grasslands, scrublands, redwood forests, streams, ponds, and historic buildings.

A wheat field ready for harvest

Farms and ranches, which provide our vegetables, fruit, meat, and dairy products, can also play an important role in land preservation. These "working landscapes" may not be wild, but they provide essential open space where plants grow and animals roam.

There are countless reasons to preserve the wild places of this Earth, but perhaps the most important is this: For every acre of wilderness lost, there is one less beautiful place in the world for you to explore. This land is your land—it's yours to enjoy, and it's yours to protect.

Everyone can help to protect the environment.

# To Find Out More

Here are some additional resources to help you learn more about land preservation:

 **Books**

Anderson, Peter. **John Muir: Wilderness Prophet.** Franklin Watts, 1995.

Anderson, Peter. **Gifford Pinchot: American Forester.** Franklin Watts, 1995.

Chandler, Gary, and Kevin Graham. **Protecting Our Air, Land, and Water.** Twenty First Century Books, 1996.

Petersen, David. **National Parks.** Children's Press, 2001.

Petersen, David. **Yellowstone National Park.** Children's Press, 2001.

## Organizations and Online Sites

### National Parks Conservation Association

1300 19th Street, NW
Suite 300
Washington, DC 20036
800-628-7275
*http://npca.org/flash.html*

The NPCA works with citizens and communities, businesses, landowners, and activists to protect the resources and wildlife of our national parks.

### The Nature Conservancy

4245 North Fairfax Drive
Suite 100
Arlington, VA 22203
800-628-6860
*http://nature.org/*

The Nature Conservancy works with individuals, organizations, and businesses to protect private lands worldwide.

### Theodore Roosevelt Association

*http://theodoreroosevelt. org/life/conservation.htm*

This site has links to all the national parks, monuments, national forests, and wildlife preserves created during the presidency of Theodore Roosevelt, as well as information about the conservation and land preservation laws passed by his administration.

### Yellowstone National Park

*http://nps.gov/yell/ home.htm*

This is the official National Park Service site for Yellowstone. Don't miss the Kids' Stuff link, which includes games, a Yellowstone scavenger hunt, and information on how kids can become Junior Rangers.

# Important Words

*atmosphere* the chemical gases that surround a planet

*environmentalists* people who believe that land and resources should be kept in their natural state

*national forest* an area designed for many uses, including recreation, logging, mining, and grazing

*national park* an area designed for recreation and to protect natural wonders from damage by human activities

*natural resources* materials such as air and water that are produced in nature and are valuable to humans

*pollution* the contamination of water, soil, or air by harmful chemicals

*preserve* to maintain or protect a place in its natural or historic state

# Index

# Meet the Author

Christine Petersen is a middle-school teacher who lives near Minneapolis, Minnesota. She has also worked as a biologist for the California Academy of Sciences, the U.S. Forest Service, the U.S. Geological Survey, and the Minnesota Department of Natural Resources, for which she studied the natural history and behavior of North American bats. In her free time, Christine enjoys snowshoeing, canoeing, birdwatching, and writing about her favorite wild animals and wild places. She is a member of the Society of Children's Book Writers and Illustrators and is the co-author of several True Books.